PLAY TO LIVE

*Selected Seminars
by Alan W. Watts*

Edited by
Mark Watts

and books

South Bend, Indiana

PLAY TO LIVE

and books
702 South Michigan, South Bend, Indiana 46618

Library of Congress Catalog Number: 82-072606

International Standard Book Number: 0-89708-098-X

    4 5 6 7 8 9

Printed in the United States of America

Typography by Ampersand Associates, Inc.
Chicago, Illinois

Additional copies available:
  the distributors
  702 South Michigan
  South Bend, IN 46618

PLAY TO LIVE

Dedicated to George Ingles

CONTENTS

PREFACE

My father once pointed out that his spoken word was an entirely different mode of communication than his written works; thus he preferred that his talks be heard, and his books read. However, in the nearly ten years since his passing, I have listened to several hundred hours of his recorded talks, and have found among them certain instances wherein a particular lecture or seminar session was not only notable and an original performance, but a process of realization as well. As this work originated in the spontaneous delivery of lectures to live audiences, for which Alan never prepared ahead of time, it reveals a moment-to-moment appreciation of the insights which Alan himself found in the course of his talks. It is for this reason that I have made the decision to share these examples, and in doing so have met with much encouragement.

It has been quite a challenge to adapt Alan's spoken style to the printed page, a task with which I have had the ceaseless help of my close friend, Rebecca Shropshire,

PREFACE

in transcribing, editing, and the researching of many literary references. After two years, I feel that this task has been accomplished quite successfully, and that the result is a book of contemporary significance and great impact.

Those among you who have read the works of Alan Watts before may perceive a difference in the expression of this book, as transcribed from spoken lectures, and that of Alan's other works. If, in reading, the disparity causes you to falter, may I suggest that you try reading these works aloud — perhaps among friends — to enliven within you the fascination, humor, and audacity of Alan's eloquent style of speaking.

Mark Watts

Mill Valley, California
May, 1982

1

VEIL OF THOUGHTS I

I

AN OF THOUGHTS

S omeone once suggested that thought is a means of concealing truth. Despite the fact that it is an extraordinarily useful faculty, there are an astounding number of examples showing how mankind can be bamboozled by thought. Take for instance, the use of gold as money. The confusion of money in any form whatsoever with wealth is one of the major problems from which civilization is suffering.

In our world today, when there is no technical reason whatsoever why there should be any poverty at all, the real reason poverty still exists is that people keep asking the question, "Where's the money going to come from?" They do not realize that money does not come from anywhere and never did; except, of course, if you thought it was gold. If you increased the supply of gold, and used that to finance all the world's commerce, prosperity would depend not upon finding new processes for growing food in vast quantities, or getting nutrition out of the oceans, or even water from the sun's energy.

Instead, it would depend upon discovering a new gold mine, and you can see what a nonsensical state of affairs that is! Gold is a very useful metal, especially for filling teeth, making jewelry, and maybe even covering the dome of the capital in Washington. However, the moment it is used for money and locked in vaults in the form of ingots it becomes completely useless, a false security that people cling to like an idol. It becomes like a belief in some kind of big daddy-o god with whiskers who lives above the clouds. And all this kind of belief diverts our attention from reality.

In ever so many different dimensions of life we are living in a state of total confusion between symbol and reality. We go through all sorts of rituals, but the symbols get in the way of practical life. Way back in human development when we first began to use symbols to represent the events of the physical world, we found symbolism such an ingenious device that we became completely fascinated with it. You may remember the Great Depression; one day everyone was doing business, things were going along pretty well, and the next day there were breadlines. It was as if somebody came to work and they said to him, "Sorry chum, but you can't build today. No building can go on, we don't have enough inches". And the worker said, "What do you mean, 'We haven't got enough inches'. We've got wood, haven't we? We've got metal, we've even got tape measures." And they said, "Yeah, but you don't understand the business world. We just haven't got enough inches, just plain inches. We've used too many of them." As absurd as this may seem, this is exactly what happened when we had the Depression, because money is something of the same order of reality as inches, grams, meters, pounds, or lines of latitude or longitude. It is an abstraction. It is a method of bookkeeping to obviate the cumbersome procedure of barter. But our entire culture, indeed, our entire civilization, is completely hung up on the notion that money has an independent reality of its own. This is a very striking and concrete example because it is a very serious state of affairs. Most of our political squabbles are entirely the result of being bamboozled by this thinking. It is noted that, as time goes on, the matters about which we fight are increasingly abstract, and the wars fought about abstract problems get worse and worse.

It would have been an extremely sane enterprise, looking at it from a sort of unsentimental point of view, to send the American forces to Vietnam to capture all the beautiful girls that live there and bring them back. That would, of course, be considered unworthy and base and all that sort of thing, but it would have had the advantage of leaving the country intact. We would not have wanted to kill the people because we would have wanted to capture them, and would have waged a more merciful war than we had waged in the name of abstract principle.

Today we are thinking about vast abstractions; ideologies called Communism, Capitalism, or what have you, while we are paying less and less attention to the world of physical reality, to the world of earth and trees and waters, and people. In the name of all sorts of abstractions we are busy destroying our natural environment. Wildlife, for example, is having a terrible problem continuing to exist along side human beings.

Another example of this fantastic confusion is that Congress voted a law imposing stern penalties upon anyone who should presume to burn the American Flag. They put this law through with a great deal of patriotic oratory and the quoting of poetry about Old Glory and so on, while entirely ignoring the fact that these same Congressmen, by acts of commission or omission, are burning up that for which the flag stands. They are allowing the utter pollution of our waters and of our atmosphere, the devastation of our forests, and the increasing power of the bulldozer to bring about the ghastly fulfillment of the biblical prophecy that "every valley shall be exalted, every mountain laid low". You see, they do not notice the difference between the flag and the country, the map and the territory. If you compare a physical globe and a political globe, you will see the physical one as a pretty thing with all kinds of green and brown wiggly patterns on it, but the political globe, although it still has the wiggly outlines of the land, they are all crossed over by colored patches, many of which have completely straight edges. Much of the boundary between the United States and Canada, once you get west of the Great Lakes, is simply a straight line. Yet this has little to do with anything and is actually a violation of the surface of the territory. If you look at the fair city of San Francisco, it is a lovely place. However, they planted on the hills of San Francisco a city pattern that was much more appropriate for the plains of Kansas; a grid iron. As a result, you get streets going straight up and down that are extremely dangerous. They should have followed the contours of the hills. This is a perfect example of confusing the map with the territory, of man's abstraction imposed upon physical reality.

When we use the words 'physical reality', as distinct from abstraction, what are we talking about? Philosophically, there is going to be a fight about this. If I were to say that the final reality that we are living in is the physical world, alot of people would assume that I am a materialist and that I am unspiritual because I think too much of the identification of the man with the body. If you were to open any book on yoga or Hindu philosophy, it will have within it a declaration used to begin a meditation practice which says, "I am not the body, I am not my feelings, I am not my thoughts. I am the witness who watches all this, and is not really any of it."

If I were to say, then, that the physical world is the basic reality, I would seem to be contradicting what is said in these Hindu texts. However, it all depends on just what you mean by the 'physical world'. What is it? First of all, it must be pointed out that the idea of the material world is in its own way a symbol. By analogy with the art of ceramics and pottery, alot of people think that the physical world is various forms of matter. But no one has ever been able to but their finger on anything material; that is to say, if by the word 'material' you mean some kind of basic stuff out of which the world is made. They have been able to discover various forms, various patterns, but no matter. You cannot even think how you would describe matter in some term other than form. Whenever a physicist talks about the nature of the world, he describes a form as a process which can be put into the shape of a mathematical equation. If you say, "A + B = B + A", everybody knows exactly what you mean, and it is a perfectly clear statement. Nobody needs to ask what do you mean by A or what do you mean by B. If you say, "1 + 2 = 3", that is perfectly clear. You do not need to know one what, two what, or three what.

All of our descriptions of the physical world have the nature of these formulae or numbers. They are simply mathematical patterns because what we are talking about *is* pattern. Yet, it is pattern of such a high degree of complexity that it is very difficult to deal with by thinking. In science, we are working with different ends of the spectrum of reality. We can deal with problems in which there are very few variables, or we can deal with problems in which there are almost infinitely many variables. Although, in between, we are pretty helpless. The average person cannot think through a problem involving more than three variables without a pencil in his hand. This is why, for example, it is difficult to learn complex music. Think of an organist who has two or three keyboards to work with his hands, and each hand is doing a different rhythm. With his feet on the pedals, he could be doing a different rhythm with each foot. Now, this is a difficult thing for people to learn to do, as rubbing your stomach in a circle and patting your head at the same time takes a little skill.

Most problems with which we deal in everyday life involve far more than three variables, and we are really incapable of thinking about them. Actually, the way we think about most of our problems is by simply going through the motions of thinking. We do not really think about them; we do most of our decision-making by hunch. We can collect data about a decision we have to make, but the data collected has the same sort of relation to the actual process involved in this decision as a skeleton has to a living body. It is just the bones.

There are all sorts of entirely unpredictable possibilities involved in every decision, and you do not really think about them at all. The truth of the matter is that we are as successful as we are in conducting our everyday practical lives — which is surprising, the degree to which we are successful — because our brains do the thinking for us in an entirely unconscious way. The human brain is by far more complex than any computer. The brain is, in fact, the most complex known object in the universe. Our neurologists do not really understand it; they have a very primitive conception of the brain, and they admit it. If we do not understand our own brain, that simply shows that our brains are a great deal more intelligent than we are — 'we' meaning the thing that we have identified ourselves with.

Instead of sensibly identifying ourselves with our brains, we have chosen to identify ourselves with a very small operation of the brain which is the faculty of conscious attention, a sort of radar that scans the environment for unusual features. Somehow we think we *are* that, but we are nothing of the kind. That is just a little trick we do. Actually, our brain is analyzing all sensory input all the time; analyzing all the things we do not notice, do not think about, do not even have names for. It is this marvelous, complex 'goingson' which is responsible for our being able to adapt ourselves intelligently to the rest of the physical world, and the brain is an operation of the physical world, and so, now we get back to this question of the physical world. It is a concept, simply an idea. If I were to differentiate between the physical and spiritual, I would not put the spiritual in the same class as the abstract. Most people do; they think that $1 + 2 = 3$ is a proposition of a more spiritual nature than, for example, a

tomato. I think a tomato is a lot more spiritual than
1 + 2 = 3 and this is where we really get to the point.

In Zen Buddhism when people ask, "What is the
fundamental principle of Buddhism?", you could very
well answer, "a tomato", because when you examine
the physical world you see it is really not very solid.
A tomato does not last very long; nor, for that matter,
do the things that we consider most exemplary of
physical reality, even mountains. The poet says: The
hills are shadows and they flow from form to form,
and nothing stands.

The physical world is diaphanous. It is like music.
When you play music it simply disappears, nothing is
left, and for that very reason it is one of the highest and
most spiritual of the arts. It is the most transient, also.
In a way, you might say that transiency is a mark spirituality. Alot of people think the opposite; that the
spiritual things are the everlasting things. The more a
thing tends to be permanent, the more it tends to be
lifeless. Nothing is as permanent as a diamond, and
yet, this imagery and the idea of the most mineral
objects being the most permanent, is associated with
being the most spiritual. Jesus Christ is called 'The
Rock of Ages'. Even the Buddhists have used the diamond
as an image of the fundamental reality of the universe,
but the reason for using the diamond is not that it is
hard, but that it is completely transparent. Therefore,
it affords a symbol of the void, which everything
fundamentally is. Void does not mean that there is

nothing there, but that you cannot get any idea which will sufficiently define physical reality. Every idea will be wrong, and in that sense, it will be void.

So then, in examining the physical world, we cannot even find any stuff out of which it is made. We can only recognize each other and say: "Well, I realize that I have met you before and that now I see you again", but the thing you really recognize is a consistent pattern. Let us suppose I have a rope which begins by being a manila rope, then it goes on to become a cotton rope, then it goes on with nylon, and then with silk. Now, if I tie a knot in the rope and I move the knot down along the rope, is it, as it moves along, the same knot or a different knot? We would say it is the same because we recognize the pattern of the knot; but at one point it is manila, at one point it is cotton, at another point it is nylon and at yet another it is silk. This is just like us. You are recognized by the fact that one day you face the same way as you did on the day before, and people recognize your facing. They say, "That is John Doe, or Mary Smith", but actually, the contents of your face, the water, the carbons, the chemicals, whatever they may be, are changing all the time. You are like a whirlpool in a stream. The stream is consistently whirlpooling, and we recognize the whirlpool, but the water is always moving on. We are just like that, and everything is just like that. There is nothing in the physical world that is what you may call 'substantial'. It is pattern;

that is why it is so spiritual. To be non-spiritual is not to see that. In other words, it is to impose upon the physical world the idea of 'thingness', of substantiality.

The Hindus use this idea to describe one who is involved in the concept of matter, one who identifies with the body, believing that the body is something constant, something tangible. The body, however, is really very intangible. You cannot pin it down, it is falling apart, and we are all aging, getting older. If you cling to the body you will be frustrated. The whole point is that the material world, the world of nature, is marvelous so long as you don't try to lean on it; so long as you don't cling to it. If you do not cling to it you can have a wonderful time.

Now, let us take up another very controversial issue: Many 'spiritual' people are, generally speaking, against lovemaking. Ramakrishna used to speak about the evils of women and of gold. I have already demonstrated the evils of gold, but what about the evils of women? From my point of view, women can be a source of evil if you attempt to possess them. Men can, too, for that matter. I mean, if you can say of another person, "I love you so much I want to own you and really tie you down and call you...", well, it's like the poem by Ogden Nash wherein someone claimed that he loved his wife so much that he climbed a mountain and named it after her. He named it "Mt. Mrs. Oswald McGuiness". In other words, if you try to possess, and you make your sexual passion possessive, then, in that way, you are trying to cling to the physical world. You see, others are much more interesting if you do not cling to them, if you let them be themselves and be free. In my opinion, you can have a very spiritual sex life if you aren't possessive. But on the other hand, if you are possessive, then you're in trouble. The average swami will not agree with that because he confuses the body that you touch as something evil. He is hung up with it. His attitude reminds me of the story of two Zen monks who were crossing a river. The ford was very deep because of a flood, and there was a girl who was trying to get across. One of the monks immediately picked her up, threw her over his shoulder, carried her across and put her down on the other side. Then the monks went on their way and the girl went another. Along the way, the other monk had been in a kind of embarrassed silence which he finally broke to say:

"Do you realize that you broke monastic rule by touching and picking up a woman like that?"

And the first monk said:

"Oh, but I left her on the other side of the river and you are still carrying her."

You can also find an example of this in passages where St. Paul rather irritably speaks of the opposition of the spirit and the flesh. For the Christian, you see, the word was made flesh in Christ, and there will be the resurrection of the body in the final consummation of the universe. So you cannot, really, as an orthodox Christian, take an antagonistic attitude to the flesh. Why, then, does St. Paul assume an antagonistic attitude? Well, you can only save the situation and make the New Testament consistent with itself by saying that he meant by the 'flesh' a certain kind of spiritual view of flesh as a concept. You might also talk about the 'sins of the flesh', but they have entirely to do with certain hang-ups that we have about our bodies. This, again, is what I would call leaning on the world by exploiting it. As a Buddhist, one takes the third precept, and it is usually translated: "I undertake the precept to refrain from adultery", but it doesn't say anything of the kind. Literally translated it says: "I undertake the precept not to exploit the passions." In other words, you may be bored and feeling sort of empty and at a loose end, so you think, "Well, I don't know, let's go and commit adultery, it might liven things up." This would be what they call in Zen, "Raising waves when no wind is blowing." It is quite a different matter if in a perfectly natural and spontaneous way you fall in love with someone. You are not going out of your way to get into trouble; it is appropriate and natural at the time. In the same way, instead of saying, "Let's commit adultery," many people when bored say, "Let's go eat something." They become fatter and fatter trying to fill the spiritual vacuum in their psyche with food, which doesn't do the job because it is not the function of food to fill the spiritual vacuum. In this way, one exploits the appetites, or passions. Likewise, the fifth precept, which lists the various intoxicating substances, does not say that you are not to take them; it says that you are not to get intoxicated by them. A Buddhist may drink but not get drunk.

One might say that we are confused through and through about what we mean by the material world. What I am doing here is, first of all, giving a number of illustrations which show how confused we are. So let me repeat this to get it clear. In the first place, we confuse abstract symbols, that is to say, numbers, words, and formulae, with the physical events, just as we confuse money with consumable wealth. In the second place, we confuse physical events, the whole class and category of physical events, with matter. Matter is an idea, it is a concept. It is the concept of stuff, of something solid and permanent that you can catch hold of; but you just cannot catch hold of the physical world! The physical world is the most evasive and illusive process that there is. It will not be pinned down, and therefore it fulfills all the requirements of spirit.

What I am saying is that the non-abstract physical world, which Korzybski called "unspeakable", *is* the spiritual world. The spiritual world is not something gaseous, abstract, or formless, in that sense of shapeless. It is formless in another sense. The formless world is the wiggly world. There really is no set way that the physical world is! Earlier I stated that someone once said that thoughts were made to conceal the truth. This is the fact, because there is no such thing as *the* truth that can be stated. In other words, ask the question: What is the true position of the stars in the Big Dipper? Well, it depends where you are looking at them from. There is no absolute position. In the same way, a good accountant will tell you that any balance sheet is simply a matter of opinion. There is no such thing as a true state of affairs. We are all hooked on the idea that there is an external objective world that is a certain way, and that it really is that way. History, for example, is a matter of opinion. History is an art, not a science. It is something constructed and accepted as a more or less satisfactory explanation of events which, as a matter of fact, do not have any explanation at all. Most of what happens in history is completely irrational, but people always feel that they have got to find a meaning. Let's say you get sick. You have lived a very good life and you have been helpful to other people and have done all sorts of nice things, and so you might say to the clergyman, "Why did this have to happen to me?" You are looking for an explanation when there isn't one. It just happened that way. Still, people feel very insecure if they cannot find an explanation. Why? Because they have not been able to straighten things out; the world is just not that way.

What is really going on is alot of wiggles. The way it is is always in relation to the way you are. No matter how hard I hit a skinless drum it will make no noise because the noise is the relationship between a fist and a skin. In the same way, light is the relationship between electrical energy and eyeballs. It is you who evokes the world, and you evoke the world in accordance with what kind of a 'you' you are — what kind of an organism. One organism evokes one world, another organism evokes another world, and so reality is a kind of relationship. Once you get rid of the idea of the truth as some way the world is in a fixed sense, you come to another idea of the truth altogether; the idea of truth that is God when we speak of God as the reality that exceeds all thoughts, that surpasses all definition, that is infinite, unbounded, eternal, and immeasureable in terms of time. We are not talking about a gaseous vertebrate, or a huge void without any wiggles in it. We are talking about the truth that cannot be stated, the truth that cannot be pinned down.

2

VEIL OF THOUGHTS II

H as it ever struck you that the entire intellectual venture of civilization has been a ghastly mistake? Could it be that we are now on a collision course, and that all the vaunted benefits of intelligence (ie. technology are simply going to draw the human race to an extremely swift conclusion? Of course, that might not be a bad thing, I have sometimes speculated on the idea that all stars are created out of planets, and that these planets develop high civilizations which eventually understand the secrets of nuclear energy and naturally blow themselves up. As they blow up, these stars fling out lumps of rock, which eventually spin around them and become planets all over again. Perhaps this is the actual method of genesis of the universe. This would accord with the Hindu cosmology, where time, and the events in time, are invariably looked upon as a process of progressive deterioration in which things get worse and worse as time goes on until the whole thing can't stand itself anymore and it blows itself up. Then, after a period of rest and recuperation, it begins all over again.

Why do we somehow have a distaste for a theory of time which runs in this direction? Can you even imagine a state of affairs where things are always getting better? Can anything keep going up and up forever? Of course, it is always relative. You can keep building something higher and higher, but soon you would forget where you began, and then you would see that, actually, we are always in the same place; always hoping, always thinking that the next time will be it. This is, of course, an eternal illusion.

There was a Russian philosopher who accused the Communists of converting all human beings into caryatids. As you may know, a caryatid is a pillar shaped in the human form which supports a roof. Considering the Communists and their various five-year plans, and progressive notions wherein people are always preparing for tomorrow, the Russian philosopher said to them: "You are turning all men into caryatids to support a stage upon which others will dance." His idea was that, first you have one row of caryatids supporting a floor, very soon your children are the next row of caryatids supporting another floor, and so on it goes on and on, getting higher and higher, but where did it all begin? Perhaps it would be much better to think of the future as simply deteriorating. I can explain this quite simply. Human beings are largely engaged in wasting enormous amounts of psychic energy in attempting to do things that are quite impossible to do. As the old proverb says: You cannot lift yourself up by your own bootstraps. Recently, I have come across many references in general reading and listening where people say that we just got to lift ourselves up by our bootstraps; but you can't! You can struggle and tug and pull until you are blue in the face, nothing will happen except that you exhaust yourself.

All sensible people, therefore, begin in life with two fundamental presuppositions: You are not going to improve the world, and you are not going to improve yourself. You are just what you are, and once you have accepted that you have an enormous amount of energy available to do things that *can* be done. Everyone looking at you from an external point of view will say: "My god, how much so-and-so has improved!" Hundreds of my friends are at work on enterprises to improve themselves by one religion or another, one therapy or another, this system or that system; and I am desperately trying to free people from this. I suppose that makes me a messiah of some kind, but the thing is, it cannot be done. One very simple reason is that the part of you which is supposed to improve you is exactly the same as the part of you which needs to be improved. There is not any real distinction between bad "me" and good "I", or between the higher self which is spiritual and the lower self which is animal. It is all of one piece. You are this organism, this integrated, fascinating energy pattern.

Archimedes said, "Give me a fulcrum and I will move the Earth"; but there isn't one. It is like betting on the future of the human race — I might wish to lay a bet that the human race would destroy itself by the year 2,000, but there is nowhere to place the bet. On the contrary, I am involved in the world and must try to see that it does not blow itself to pieces. I once had a terrible argument with Margaret Mead. She was holding forth one evening on the absolute horror of the atomic bomb, and how everybody should spring into action and abolish it, but she was getting so furious about it that I said to her: "You scare me because I think you are the kind of person who will push the button in order to get rid of the other people who were going to push it first". So she told me that I had no love for my future generations, that I had no responsibility for my children, and that I was a phoney swami who believed in retreating from facts. But I maintained my position. As Robert Oppenheimer said a short while before he died, "It is perfectly obvious that the whole world is going to hell. The only possible chance that it might not is that we do *not* attempt to prevent it from doing so." You see, many of the troubles going on in the world right now are being supervised by people with very good intentions whose attempts are to keep things in order, to clean things up, to forbid this, and to prevent that. The more we try to put everything to rights, the more we make fantastic messes. Maybe that is the way it has got to be. Maybe I should not say anything at all about the folly of trying to put things to right but simply, on the principle of Blake, let the fool persist in his folly so that he will become wise.

This, then, may be said to be an argument against all kinds of do-gooding. Perhaps you should not take me too seriously, but I am pitching a case for the fact that civilization may have been a mistake; that it would be much better to leave everything alone, and that the wild animals are wiser than we in that they, putting it in our crude and not very exact language, follow their own instincts. If a moth mistakes a flame for the signal on which it gets a mating call and flies into the flame, so what! A moth does not worry, it does not go buzzing around in a state of anxiety wondering whether this sex call is the real thing or just a flame. Nor does it think consciously about the future, and therefore, it is not troubled. The species of moths goes on and on, and so far as we know, they have been around for an incredibly long time. Maybe even longer than we have. Bees, ants, and creatures of this kind have long since escaped from history. They live a settled existence — one which you might consider rather boring simply because it does not have constant change in the way we do. They live the same rhythm again and again and again, but because they do not bother to remember it consciously it never gets boring. Because they do not bother to predict, they are never in a state of anxiety; yet they survive. We who predict, "We who look before and after", as Emerson says, and we who are always concerned as to whether this generation is going to be better or worse than the one that came before, we are tormented. Because of this tremendous preoccupation with time, we do not realize how beautiful we are, in spite of ourselves.

The conscious radar is a trouble-shooter, it is always on the lookout for variation in the environment which may bring about disaster. Our conscious attention is from one day to the next entirely preoccupied with time and with planning, with what has been and with what will be. Since trouble-shooting is its function, we then get the feeling that man is born to trouble. We ignore, in this preoccupation with conscious attention, how marvelously we get on; how, for most of the time, our physical organs are in a fantastically harmonious relationship, and how our body relates by all sorts of unconscious responses to the physical environment. If you became aware of all the adjustment processes that are being managed spontaneously and subconsciously by your organism you would find yourself in the middle of great music. This, of course, occasionally happens.

The mystical experience is nothing other than becoming aware of your true physical relationship to the universe. You are amazed, thunderstruck by the feeling that, underneath everything that goes on in this

world, and the fundamental thing is a state of unbeliev-
able bliss. Why not? Why else would there be anything
happening? If the "game isn't worth the candle", if the
universe is basically nothing but a tormented struggle,
why have one? Hasn't it ever struck you that it would
be much simpler not to have any existence? It would re-
quire no effort, there would be no problems, so why
is there anything going on? Let me say not *why* but
how is there anything going on? If it is all fundamentally
a drag, what reason could there be for its being? Everything would have committed suicide long ago and be at
rest. "Aboo, Ben Adhem, may his tribe decrease by
cautious birth control and be at peace".

We might work on this possibility, then, that
civilization has been a mistake, that we have taken
completely the wrong track and should have left things
to nature. Of course, this is the same problem that is
brought up in the book of Genesis. Actually, the Fall of
Man in Genesis is his venture into technology. In the
Bible, the Hebrew words for the knowledge of good
and evil are connected with technics, with what is
technically expeditious and what is not. Actually, the
words are connected with metallurgy. When you eat of
the fruit of the tree of knowledge, and you become
as God, you think you are going to control your own
life. God says, "Okay, baby, you want to be God,
you try it! But the trouble with you is you've got a
one-tracked mind, and therefore you cannot be God.

To be God, you have to have an infinitely many-tracked mind." — which is, of course, what our brain has. The brain is infinitely many-tracked, but conscious attention is not, it is one-tracked. As we say, you can only think of one thing at a time, and you cannot take charge of the universe with that kind of consciousness because there is too much of it, too many variables. This is why, for example, people consult the *I Ching*, the Book of Changes. If you are tossing a coin to make decisions, (and everybody does fundamentally make their decisions by tossing a coin), is it not better to have a 64-sided coin than a two-sided coin? The *I Ching* gives you 64 possibilities of approach to any given decision instead of just two, yes or no. It is based on yes or no, however, because it is based on the yang and the yin. In the same way, digital computers use a number system which consists only of the figures zero and one out of which you can construct any number. This system was invented by Leibnitz, who also saw it in the Book of Changes, an amazing book that is somehow always with us. It is, then, a way of helping your own multi-variabled brain arrive at decisions in cooperation with your own mind, much like a Roschach blot. The *I Ching* uses very laconic remarks into which everyone reads just exactly what they want to read. You might even come to the conclusion that it helps in making a decision because you do not have to accept responsibility for it. You might say, "It told me". Much in the same way, when you go to a guru, you might say, "My guru is very wise, and he has instructed me to do this", but it was *you* who decided on this guru. How did you know he was a good one? After all, you gave him his authority because you picked him out. It always comes back to you, but we like to pretend that it doesn't.

The point is that one's conscious attention is not oneself; oneself is everything underneath. One's conscious attention has about the same relation to oneself as the bookkeeping does to a business. If you are selling groceries, there is very little resemblance between your books and the goods that move over your shelves and counters. The bookkeeping is merely a record of it, as is our reflective consciousness.

Suppose we follow the argument, then, that we have made a mistake in bringing about civilization, and that now we are not going to survive. There are various things that can be said about this. Just as I have speculated that all stars used to be planets, one could ask, "Is it such a good thing to survive?" You may remember the passage in T.S. Eliot's *Wasteland* which says: "This is the way the world ends, not with a bang but a whimper." Yet, some people would rather end with a bang than a whimper. Some people prefer a kind of potlatch situation where they have a huge fire that goes out in a hurry, while others prefer to burn their fire very gradually, conserving fuel, and just keeping enough heat going so that they last a long time. Which do you prefer? Do you want to be a tortoise that lives for hundreds of years but drags itself around very slowly, or would you rather be a little humming-bird that dances and lives at a terrific pace? You cannot say one is right and the other is wrong. Just so, there may be nothing wrong with the idea of a world or a civilization that lives at a terrific, increasing pace of change, and then explodes. That may be perfectly okay.

My point is, if we could reconcile ourselves to the notion that this is perfectly okay, then we would be less inclined to push that button. If you cannot stand anxiety, if you simply cannot be content for issues to be undecided, then you are liable to push the button because you would say, "Let's get it over with."

Let us say, then, that maybe civilization really was not a mistake, that it was just as natural as anything else. We are a being that exists under conditions of illusion, that imagines it is controlling its own destiny, which thinks that it is capable of improving itself, and by virtue of this illusion, destroys itself rapidly in an interesting way. Let us suppose this is what we are, but we still come back to the point that we are spending an enormous amount of energy in doing things that cannot be done, like tugging on our own bootstraps. If you find this frustrating, if you really do not like it, you don't have to do it; you *can* stop.

An interesting paradox is that when you stop trying to do what cannot be done, you become happier and more energetic. People always wondered about the Calvinists because the Calvinists believed that from the beginning of time God had pre-ordained who was to be saved and who was to be damned, and that one simply does not have a choice. This is pre-destination, and the logical assumption would be, therefore, that these people would just sit, and wait, and say, "There is nothing we can do about it." However, the Calvanists were very different than that. They were very energetic people (perhaps too energetic) who gave us the Protestant ethic. They were vigorously moral, but because they believed in pre-destination they had all the psychic energy available for living that the Catholics were dissipating wondering whether they were saved or not. Calvinists did not waste their energy trembling in a state of fear wondering, "have I made the right decision?"

In this day and age we say in psychiatry, or in most schools of psychotherapy, that it is important for you to accept yourself rather than to be in conflict. "Get with yourself", they say. Still, no one dares to take this thing too far. There is always a little bit of reservation that goes with it. I have never heard a preacher give a sermon on the passage which begins: "Be not anxious for the morrow." Occasionally they refer to it, but they say, "Well, that's all very well for Jesus." The actual putting into practice of this, few will agree with. More often they say it is not practical; but it *is* practical. It is much more practical than what we are doing, if by the word practical you mean that it has survival value.

All of this is a kind of two-sided process. The first step is not being anxious for the morrow, and the second is not dreaming for one moment that you can change anything or improve anything. Which of you by being anxious can add one cubit to his stature? Like the belief in predestination, this has an unexpected consequence; namely, the making of energy available so that you can take care of the morrow for the simple reason that you are no longer worrying about it today. Thus it comes about that people who do not live for the morrow have a reason to make plans. Those who live for the morrow have no reason to make plans for anything. They never catch up with tomorrow because they do not live in the present. Instead, they plan for a future which never arrives, and this is very stupid.

I would like to make clear that all this is said in quite another spirit than the spirit of sermonizing. I am not talking at all about something you *should* do. All that I am doing is explaining a situation. You can do anything you like about it. You actually cannot lift yourself up by your bootstraps, however hard you might try. I am merely pointing out that it cannot be done. I am not saying that you shouldn't try, because it may be your lifestyle to constantly be attempting to do things that cannot be done. I do this, in a way, just as all poets do it. A poet is always trying to describe what cannot be said. He gets close, he even gives the illusion that he has made it. This is a great art; to say what cannot be said. I am trying to express the mystical experience, and it just cannot be done. Instead, I am weaving a tapestry of intricate nonsense patterns which seem as if they were about to make sense, but everything I am telling you is really a very elaborate deception.

I was once talking with Fritz Perls at the Esalen Institute, and he said to me, "The trouble with you is you're all words. Why don't you practice what you preach?" So I said to him, "I don't preach. And furthermore, don't put words down because the patterns that people make with words are just like the patterns of ferns or of the marks on sea shells. They are a dance, and they are just as much a legitimate form of life as flowers." And he said, "You're impossible."

But all of this is very important, and it is why, in certain methods of meditation and religious rituals, we use words in a way that is not ordinarily in accord with the use of words. Words are normally used to convey information, but, in many religious rituals, words are used musically for the sake of sound. In this way, one can liberate oneself from enthrallment with words. If you take any ordinary word like "body" and say it once, it seems to be quite sensible, but say it four or five times: "body, body, body, body, ...", then you think, "what a funny noise". Or say: "apple-dumpling, apple-dumpling, apple-dumpling . . . . . ". It's kind of a nice sound.

This is one of the great methods of meditation, called mantra yoga, which uses sound for liberating consciousness. You can take all sorts of nonsense, chant it, and concentrate on the sounds quite apart from anything they may mean. For this reason, the Catholic Church made a great mistake in deciding to celebrate Mass in the vernacular. Now everyone knows what it means and that it really was not so hot after all. Before, it was completely incomprehensible and had a sense of mystery to it, and if you knew how to use these words as a sadhana, a method of meditation, you could do very well with them. When monks are trained to recite the Divine Office, the teacher explains to the novice, "Don't think about the meaning of the words. Just say the words with your mouth, and keep your consciousness on the presence of God." By using words in this way you overcome the slavery to words. I have written a book of nonsense diddies to be used in this way. You get the rhythm going, as an incantation, and it becomes a way of getting beyond the bondage of thought. You cannot think without words, but if you preoccupy your consciousness with meaningless words, they can stop your thought process. Then, you simply dig the sound. Do you know what it is to dig the sound of anything? Anyone who has had a psychedelic experience knows exactly what this means. I can only say that you go down into it, and into it, and into it, until suddenly you realize that the vibration you are listening to, or singing, is what there is. This is the energy of the cosmos. This is what is going on.

Everything is a kind of pulsation of energy which in Zen Buddhism is called 'suchness' or 'thatness' — *tathata*. That is what we are all doing. Only, we look around, and here we all are — people. We have got faces on, and we talk, and we are supposed to be making sense, but actually we are just going, "Da-da-da, da-da-da, da-da-da-da-da", in a very complicated way. We are playing this life game, and if we not get with it, it passes us by. And that is alright. If you miss the bus that is your privelege. But it really is a great deal more fun to go with the dance, and to know that is what you are doing, instead of agonizing about the whole thing. Life is something that simply keeps happening. I know that we are all very unique, but if you concentrate and look too closely, you get myopic about the uniqueness of each individual and say, "What a shame, that is never going to happen again". On the other hand, if you came to Earth from Mars, everyone would look the same, and you wouldn't even be able to tell the difference between men and women. You would say, "Well, this is definitely something that keeps happening." It all depends on what level of magnification you are looking at, and where you are putting your values.

3

VEIL OF THOUGHTS III
Divine Madness

I would like to indulge in the discussion of a particularly virulent and dangerous form of divine madness called "falling in love"; which is, from a practical point of view, one of the most insane things you can do, or that can happen to you. In the eyes of a given woman or a given man, an opposite, who though to the eyes of everyone else is a perfectly plain and ordinary person, can appear to be a god or goddess incarnate; to be such an enchantment that one can say, in the words of an old song that probably dates me, "Every little breeze seems to whisper Louise." This can be seen as a strangely disruptive and subversive experience in the conduct of human affairs because you never know when it will strike, or for what reason. Once you get into it, it is something like contracting a very chronic disease, and we sometimes try to resolve it by making it the basis for a marriage, which is an extraordinarily dangerous thing to do.

Western civilization has a curious tradition of the family which seems to be the most ridiculous composition of disparate ideas imaginable. When we go back to its origins in the Hebrew and Christian traditions, we find that the idea of marriage and the experience of falling in love are really rather separate things. In early agrarian cultures, no one ever chose their marriage partner. There are, of course, exceptions to this, and in the history of ancient Greece you occasionally find a woman who is called a *parthenos*, which has been mis-translated to "virgin". The correct meaning of *parthenos* is a woman who chooses her own husband, and it therefore, has nothing strictly to do with a virgin, although, a woman who chooses her own husband might conceivably be a virgin.

By and large, however, a marriage was an alliance of families. It was contracted not simply for the purpose of raising children, but also to create a social unit smaller than a village. The elders had an enormous voice in who their children were going to marry; and they would dicker amongst themselves and use go-betweens in considering not only whether this girl was suitable for their son, or visa versa, but also what kind of dowry she would bring, and whether it would be advantageous to the families to form such an alliance. Of course, until quite recent times, these things were always important in the marital affairs of royal families. As it is notorious, almost all royal families kept concubines and had outside arrangements when and if the king or queen should happen to fall in love, and this simply prevented monogamy from becoming monotony. That is why, to this day, marriage is a civil or religious ceremony, the basis of which is a legal contract where one signs on the dotted line. There are all kinds of laws that relate to contracts, and this contract is a particularly difficult one to get out of.

The rationale for this is quite obvious: society requires a secure environment for children, but also simply because it prefers to encourage the general stability of things. When people break up a marriage it is sort of unnerving for everyone. You see a couple and you think for a very long time that they are the happiest and most well-adjusted couple you have ever met. The next thing you know they have split up. You begin to see people breaking up all around and you think, "Now what goes on here? Are all my friends crazy? (Interestingly enough, we call it 'breaking up', as though something precious had been smashed; but depending in how you evaluate it, it might be something different altogether).

Into the feudal conception of marriage there came what was called 'The Cult of Courtly Love', which was largely a result of the poetic movement centered in Southern France during the Middle Ages — although its exact origin is something which scholars dispute. According to one theory, the knight or courtly lover, who was also a poet, would select a lady to be his heart's desire — preferably a married lady — and he would yearn for her, sing songs under her window, and send her messages with little tokens of his devotion. But, according to this one theory, he could never go to bed with her. Not only would that have been adultery, but it would have spoiled the state of being in love. The state of being in love was to always be in an unfulfilled and unhappy state. (This is the theory of Dennis deRougemont in his book, *Love in the Western World*, or *Passion is Society*. It has two different titles).

This second theory is probably more realistic: It holds that the greatest ladies of the noble families were awfully bored because their husbands were always out hunting, making war, wenching, and so on. The ladies felt they had to have lovers too, and one can see why a great deal of poetry arose out of all this. My friend, Yanko Varda, always said that laws about sexual relationships should never be liberalized. He felt that there should always be strict disapproval of adultery and fornication because if it isn't difficult to attain, it isn't as much fun. In my book, *Beyod Theology*, I have worked out a whole theory of the Christian repression of sex, stating that the secret intent was to make people more interested in sex. If there were complete liberality and promiscuity in every direction, it would all become so easy that it might, indeed, be in danger of becoming a bore. Then people would seek other dissipations of perhaps a less healthy kind.

So then, as a result of the gradual fusion of these two approaches to the realtionship of the sexes — the family alliance and the perpetual romance — we arrive at the idea of the romantic marriage in which the two trends are mis-allied, to say the very least. Herein, a person is supposed to fall in love with someone of their own choice (and naturally it has to be that way if you are going to fall in love), and then one must enter into that relationship with a legal contract in which you stand before a magistrate or a priest and so solemnly curse and swear that you will be faithful to each other until death do you part — which sometimes leads to murder.

It seems to me perfectly obvious that if two young people who are extremely anxious to get into each other's embraces have only one way of doing so, which under the circumstances is to enter into this contract, they will naturally be ready to promise anything to fulfill this desire. While there are indeed many legally married couples who have very happy alliances that goes on all of their lives, we do not hear about them because good news is never news. Only the unhappy couples make the newspapers, and there are an enormous number of them.

So far as I know there is no way of *making* a marriage work. Every attempt to make a marriage work, secretly, within the breast of each partner, builds up hostility. I know about this as I am speaking from a certain amount of bitter experience. You can work very hard to keep a marriage together, and as you do so you may fail to recognize that you are being untrue to your own emotions. You might think, "Well, I must control my own emotions for the sake of the children, and for the sake of society." So you work on it, and work on it, and one of the ways of working on it is to try to convince yourself that you are in love. You may go through the pretense of love and you may hypnotize yourself with loving language towards your partner. You might go out of your way to make little lists to remember attentions you must pay, to keep a diary in which you note your wedding anniversary because you are very liable to forget it. Nevertheless, the more you work at it, the more you are building up promises and expectations for something which you are probably not going to come through with at the level of deep feeling. Everyone is well aware of this, and you know it in the back of your mind, and so you increasingly build yourself into a wall-to-wall trap. The mutual hostility grows worse and worse, such that one psychologist was recently known to ask a patient, "With whom are you in love against?"

Indeed, the most awkward form of falling in love occurs between people who are already married to someone else. This is invariably a cataclysmic and disruptive experience in our present social order. Today there are many people still living out Victorian novels in which the great thing is when two people who are madly in love with each other say, "Well, it is best for

us not to see each other anymore", and so this fantastically mad experience of love is denied, swept under
the rug, and strangled. What should one do?

As I have often said, I am not a preacher, and
I therefore do not know what one *should* do. But I
would like to reflect a bit more on this particular form
of madness, and to raise again a very disturbing question: Is it only when you are in love with another
person that you see them as they really are? In the
ordinary way, when you are not in love with a person,
could it be that you see only a fragmented version of
that being? When you are in love with someone, you
do indeed see them as a divine being. Now, suppose
that is what they truly are and that your eyes have
by your beloved been opened, in which case your
beloved is serving to you as a kind of guru. This is
the reason why there is a form of sexual yoga which is
based upon the idea that man and woman are to each
other as a mutual guru and student. Through a tremendous outpouring of psychic energy in total devotion
and worship for this other person, who is respectively
god or goddess, you realize, by total fusion and contact,
the divine center in them. At once it bounces back to
you and you discover your own.

I do not regard falling in love as just a sexual
infatuation because it is always more than that. When
you fall in love it is a much more serious involvement.
You simply cannot forget this person. You feel miserable
when not in their presence and you are always yearning

and saying, "Let's see more of each other. Let's get together. We are completely entangled". Here we have introduced what I will call a spiritual element. The Hindus were sensible enough to realize that sexual intercourse was a means of awakening and enlightenment, and therefore, it was surrounded with a sort of religious ritual and meditative art. Sexual yoga is designed to allow the feelings of mutual love, which are the extent of grand passion, to be an extremely fitting fulfillment and expression.

Ordinarily, most sexual intercourse is a matter of wham-bam-and-thank-you-mam. It does not go on for very long, and so the passions discharge very quickly. Sexual yoga is what might be called contemplative sex, as distinct from active sex. Statues have been found on the walls of Hindu temples and in Tibetan shrines that have a figure, usually in the accourtrements of a bodhisattva or buddha, sitting in the lotus posture with a feminine counterpart wrapped around him. They are in complete contact, not so much kissing as touching noses or looking straight into each other's eyes, but they are in sexual union. In this sort of posture, (and it takes a light girl), it is rather difficult to wiggle, so they stay quite still. While in this posture, the feeling of the intensity of love builds up a tremendous electrical energy such that they are actually aware an exchange of forces that can be described as a sensation of the 'one' physically melting into the 'other'. This union may last for a very long time, and in this way it touches dimensions of personal relationship and interchange that we do not ordinarily have with anyone. The point of it is that by having such deep union with a woman, a man completes his nature, as does a woman with a man.

Every man has a feminine element and every woman has a masculine element. An integrated person is one in whom both are developed. For this reason, when you read about the physical characteristics of a buddha or a bodhisattva, you will find that you are reading a physical description of an androgynous being. It is never mentioned in textbooks, but a buddha is supposed to have a retractable penis like a cat. This symbolizes that his genital organ is simultaneously male and female. Now this is something which contains a very important message for our Western culture because here we have a cult machismo; the cult of the all-male man. Naturally, as a counterpart of that we have the all-woman woman, typified by the frilly-fluffy kind, or the overly dramatic type who is frantically jealous and makes love with her nails in your back. Between the all male-male and the all woman-woman, there is simply no possibility for relationship. They have nothing in common.

In the average suburban American home when there is a cocktail party, or any social juxtaposition of the sexes, you very quickly see that all the wives gather at one end of the patio and all the husbands gather at the other end to talk their respective forms of shop. This is particularly because the American male, especially the blue collar male and a certain type of business male, is very much afraid of sharing any feminine characteristics; whether they be external movements and clothing or internal feelings, they are reluctant to show tenderness. It is possible that they are afraid of developing their femininity because that might lead them to homosexuality. Many men are so terrified of this that they cultivate an exterior of tough masculinity. They often become the sort of people who readily volunteer to be sergeants in the Marine Corps, police officers, bouncers, test pilots, and various Hemmingway types. We have an enormous number of them, and sometimes young men who are the children of these types realize their fathers are pretty mixed up. Suddenly they start growing their hair long or going around in outlandish costumes full of color, and everybody in the old culture is scared to death that all their sons are becoming queers.

So then, to return to the main stream of this problem: falling in love is a thing that strikes like lightening and is, therefore, extremely analagous to the mystical vision. We do not really know how people obtain the mystical vision, and there is not as yet a very clear rationale as to why it happens. However, we do know that it happens to many people who never did anything to look for it. Many people, especially in adolescence, have suddenly had the mystical vision without any warning, and with no previous interest in this kind of thing. On the other hand, many people who have practiced yoga or zen disciplines for years and years have never seen it. In both classes, of course, there are exceptions. There are those who have had this experience spontaneously, and there are those who through the practice of yoga or zen have attained it. As yet, we are not clear as to why it comes about, or if there is any method of attaining it. The best approach seems to be to give up the whole idea of getting it because it is quite unpredictable, and like falling in love, it is capricious, and therefore crazy.

If you should be so fortunate as to encounter either of these experiences, it seems to me to be a total denial of life to refuse it. What we have to admit in our society, so that we can contain this kind of madness, is a far more realistic marriage arrangement that can contain the possibility of falling in love. If you go into it as a love affair which may simply be hot pants, to then set up a family in which each person expects of the other to always be in love with them, then, if in that context you fall in love with someone else, it is out of necessity disruptive of the marriage and of the family. If marriage were based more on the old idea of the reasonable contract between two people who wish to bring up children, who are expected to at least be good friends, and who can allow each other to have their own freedom; then, when love strikes it can be tolerated within this arrangement; provided you are not to be so unreasonable as to go on and think, "Well, since I have fallen in love with someone else, I must marry them" — that would be totally ridiculous.

We *can* structure the necessary, stable, social institution of a family without it being constantly threatened of floundering on the rocks of love. When people marry and they take any vows at all to each other, they say they will always be true to each other, usually in the sense of meaning, "I will always love you". If instead they meant, "I will always be truthful to you and I will not pretend that my feelings towards you are other than what they are", then marriage could be an arrangement that would set people free. You would say: "I marry you because I think you are a reasonable person to live with, and therefore, I want you to be you. I don't want you to be someone else. I don't want you to be a rubber stamp of me — think how boring that would be."

Marriage should be an alliance of two people who cooperate with each other in certain ways. If it should so occur that they are of immense sexual attraction to each other, so much the better, but this should not be the primary factor in entering into marriage. Admittedly, you must be to a certain extent attracted to each other, otherwise there would be no progeny. This seems to me to be a sensible and reasonable view, and because it is sensible and reasonable, it can accomodate what is not sensible and reasonable, which is falling in love. We should regard marriage, especially if it is to be called 'holy matrimony', as a mutual setting free of two people to live together in freedom, and therefore, in responsibility. The present situation, although it is pretending to be responsible, is extremely irresponsible because it is allowing dishonesty with respect to the way you feel toward another person.

Interestingly, we say 'falling' into love, and not 'rising' into love. Love is an act of surrender to another person; it is total abandonment. In love you give yourself over, you let go, and you say, "I give myself to you. Take me, do anything you like with me." To many people this seems quite mad because it means letting things get out of control, and all sensible people keep things in control. So, is it sensible to find security through vigilance, police and guards? Watch it! Who is going to watch the guards? Actually, the course of wisdom, what is really sensible, is to let go, to commit oneself, to give oneself up; and this is considered quite mad. It is thus that we are driven to the strange conclusion than in madness lies sanity.

4

BEING IN THE WAY

The development of self-consciousness and the ability to reflect on one's own knowledge is the great human predicament — it is simultaneously a blessing and a curse. To be happy and to know you are happy is the cup of life overflowing, but there is of course the reverse to this which is to be miserable and to know you are miserable. I am often reminded of the limerick:

> *There was a young man who said:*
> *"Though it seems that I know that I know,*
> *What I would like to see, is the I that knows me,*
> *When I know, that I know, that I know."*

One can see how a person, by becoming too aware of himself, can get in the way of his own existence. The Taoists have a way of dealing with this problem. They practice what is called 'fasting the heart', which is connected with the idea of being empty. In Chinese, this word for heart does not mean heart in the physiological sense, it means heart-mind. A person who has *mushin*, no mind or heart, is a very high order of person. It means that their psychic center does not get in its own way. It operates as if it were not there.

The Taoist philosopher, Chuang-tzu wrote:

When the geese fly over the water,
And are reflected in the water,
The geese do not intend to cast their reflection,
And the water has no mind to retain their image.

This is the fundamental Taoist idea of being absent as a condition of being present. For as Chuang-tzu noted:

When your belt is comfortable you do not feel it,
When your shoes are comfortable it is as if you
were not wearing any.

This same principle is presented in Lao-tzu's *Tao Te Ching*, which was written for several purposes, but is primarily a book of wisdom for governors. You may take it as a guide to mystical law, but principally it was an introduction to the art of ruling. Suppose the President of the United States were as unknown to you as the local sanitary inspector, or the man who looks after the drains and sewage disposal. This is not a glamorous figure, but for that very reason he probably does his job more efficiently than the President. Perhaps if the President were someone quite anonymous, one whom we did not have to think about, he would be a very good ruler. In just the same way, for example, unless you are sick you do not have to attend to the government of your own body. It happens automatically. It goes on day after day and the better it is, the less you have to think about it, and the less you think about it the better it is.

The second word in the title of the *Tao Te Ching, te,* is ordinarily translated as virtue; as in the healing virtues of a plant. It means the excellence of things in the sense that a tree excels at being a tree, and nobody really knows how it does it. There is no way of imitating a tree. The only way is to be one. So, in the same way, when a human being shows extraordinary skill at something, they excel in it naturally.

Te is a way of talking about a human being who has learned to live in harmony with the Tao. It is like a situation in which we are floating in a river and the river keeps carrying us along. Some of the people in the river are swimming against it, but they are still being carried along. Others have learned that the art of the thing is to swim with it, and they are carried along too. The only difference is that those swimming with the river know they are being carried along, but the people who are swimming against it think they are swimming in the opposite direction. Really they are not. You can swim against the river and pretend not to be flowing with it, but you still are. A person who is no longer making the pretense, however, who knows that he must go with the river, suddenly acquires, behind everything that he does, the force of the river.

The whole river is behind him and he can subtly direct his course as a ship can use its rudder, or more skillfully still, as a sailboat uses the wind. When a sailboat tacks and goes in a direction contrary to the wind, it is still using the wind to blow it along. The art of sailing is Taoism in perfection. It is a highly skillful art. The man who rows a boat uses effort, but the man who has the intelligence to put up a sail uses the magic of nature.

I remember once I was looking in the open air and one of those glorious little thistle-down things came floating by. I reached up and brought it down and it looked as if it were struggling to get away, as if I caught an insect by one leg. At first I thought, "Well, it's not really doing that, it's just the wind blowing it." But then I thought again, "Really? Only the wind blowing it? Surely it is the structure of this thing which in cooperation with the existence of wind enables it to move like an animal; but using the wind's effort, not its own."

In this way, the meaning of *te* is that kind of intelligence which, without your using very much effort, gets everything to cooperate with you. One example is never forcing other people to agree with you, but giving them the notion that the idea you wanted them to have was their own. This is preeminently a feminine art, but anyone who really wants a lover learns to cultivate it. The secret is never to pursue the other person because then you will appear too aggressive and they will think you are obviously someone who has had difficulty in finding lovers before, and therefore, you must have some undesirably awful thing about you. If you are slightly difficult to get, however, they somehow get the idea that you are a highly prized object and so they pursue. It is the same way when you want to teach a baby to swim. One thing you can do is to put the baby in the water with you and start swimming backwards, creating a vacuum. This pulls the baby along. In both cases, the principle is the same, and if you have patience, you can always do this.

In this state of being in accord with Tao, the effortless flow of nature, there is a certain feeling of weightlessness which is similar to the weightlessness that people feel when they get into outer space, or when they go deep into the ocean. In these instances there is the sensation that you are not carrying your body around, like the Taoist sage, Lieh-tzu, who had a reputation for being able to ride on the wind. As Chuang-tzu says,

It is easy to stand still, the difficulty
  is to walk without touching the ground.

Likewise, when Suzuki was asked what it is like to have satori he said:

It is just like ordinary everyday experience
  except about two inches off the ground.

What is this weightlessness? In one sense it means that you are not moving around in constant opposition to yourself. Most people are in constant opposition to themselves because they think that they must be in control. When the human being developed the power to be aware of himself, to know that he knows, and man had the sensation of being in charge, he got anxious. This was the Fall of Man. This was when he first started asking himself, "Have I done all that should be done?", "Have I taken enough factors into consideration?", "Am I aware enough of myself?" As Lao-tzu says, "When the great Tao was lost, there came 'duty to man' and right conduct'." This is to say that nobody talks about how you ought to behave unless things have gone radically wrong. There can be no conception of faithful ministers of State unless there are a lot of lousy politicians around. There is constantly in the tradition of Taoism the idea that all moral preaching is confusion. There was an alleged conversation between Confucius and Lao-tzu in which Lao-tzu asked Confucius to explain what is charity and duty to one's neighbor. Confucius gave him a little sermon on giving up one's interest and working for others, whereupon Lao-tzu said:

> *What stuff! Sir, regard the universe.*
> *The stars come out invariably every night.*
> *The sun rises and sets, the birds flock*
>   *and migrate without exception,*

All flowers and trees grow upwards
without exception.
You, by your talk of charity and duty to one's
neighbor, you are just introducing confusion
into the empire.
Your attempt to eliminate self is a positive
manifestation of selfishness.
You are like a person beating a drum in search of
a fugitive.

All talk about selflessness, about being virtuous, or enlightened, or integrated, or self-actualized or non-neurotic, attests to the fact that it has not happened, and will in fact stand in the way of its happening.

There is an amusing story about Lieh-tzu hearing of a very great master and going to study with him. The master lived in a small hut, and Lieh-tzu would sit outside the hut, but the master paid no attention to him. (This is the way with Taoist masters, they do not want students because they feel they have nothing to teach.) After a year of sitting outside the hut, Lieh-tzu was fed up with waiting so he went away. Soon he got very regretful about this and thought he really should make a try so he went back to the master, who said, "Why this ceaseless coming and going?" So Lieh-tzu sat there again and tried to control his mind in such a way that he would not think of the differences between gain and loss. The point, you see, is to try to live in such a way that everything is neither an advantage nor a disadvantage.

There is another story which makes this point quite clearly:

> *Once upon a time there was a Chinese farmer whose horse ran away, and all the neighbors came around to commiserate that evening, saying, "So sorry to hear your horse has run away. That's too bad."*
>
> *And the farmer said, "Maybe."*
>
> *The next day the horse came back bringing seven wild horses with it and everybody came around that evening and said, "Oh, isn't that lucky! What a wonderful turn of events, you now have eight horses!"*
>
> *And the farmer said, "Maybe."*
>
> *The next day the farmer's son tried to break one of these horses to ride, but was thrown off and broke his leg. And all the neighbors came around and said, "Oh, dear, that's too bad."*
>
> *And the farmer said, "Maybe."*
>
> *The following day the conscription officers came around to draft people into the army and they rejected his son because he had a broken leg.*
>
> *All the people came around again and said, "Isn't that just great!"*
>
> *And the farmer said, "Maybe."*

This story illustrates the attitude of not thinking of things in terms of gain or loss, advantages or disadvantages, because you never really know. We never know whether something is fortune or misfortune, we only know the momentary changes as they alter our sense of hope about things. A Taoist is wise enough to understand that there isn't any fixed good or bad, and so his point of view is what is called 'non-choosing'. Lieh-tzu attempted to keep his mind in a state of non-choosing, and it is a very difficult thing to overcome one's habits of feeling and thinking in this respect. After Lieh-tzu had practiced this for a year, the master looked at him, sort of recognized he was there, and after another year's practice he invited him to come and sit inside his hut. Then something changed in Lieh-tzu and he did not try anymore to control his mind. What he did, he put in this way:

> I let my ears hear whatever they wanted to hear.
> I let my eyes see whatever they wanted to see.
> I let my feet move wherever they wanted to go,
> and I let my mind think whatever it wanted to think.

Then he said it was a very strange sensation because all his bodily existence seemed "to melt and become transparent and have no weight, and I did not know whether I was walking on the wind or the wind was walking on me." That is what is meant by 'fasting the heart'. In the ordinary way we say, "Well, that made quite an impression on me", as if you were a slate or a blackboard upon which life makes an impression. We say, "Here are all these events, I am the observer, I remember them, and they make an impression on me."

But in the psychology of Taoism there is no difference between 'you' as observer and whatever it is that you observe. The only thing that is you is the observation of life from a certain point of view. We create an opposition between the thinker and the thought, the experiencer and the experience, the knower and the known. This is because we think about knowledge in terms of certain metaphors such as the stylis on the writing sheet, or as the reflection in the mirror. All of these kinds of images come into our idea of knowledge.

The Taoist theory of knowledge is quite different. There is not a knower facing the known. It would be more like saying that if there is any knower at all it contains the known. Your mind is not in your head, your head is in your mind. Your mind, understood from the point of view of vision, is space. All that we call space contains the myriads of shapes and colors. It does not reflect them as a mirror, but it is the absense which guarantees their presence, and it is their presence which guarantees its absence.

Differences, borders, lines, surfaces, and boundaries do not really divide things from each other at all; they join them together. All boundaries are held in common. When you understand this, you see that the sense of being 'me' is exactly the same sensation as being one with the whole cosmos. You do not need to go through some other weird, different, or odd kind of experience to feel in total connection with everything. Once you get the clue, you see that the sense of unity is inseparable

from the sense of difference. The secret is that what is
'other' eventually turns out to be you. That is the element
of surprise in life — to find the thing that is most
alien to you. If you go out at night and look at the stars
you will realize that they are millions and millions and
billions of miles away — vast configurations out in
space! You can lie back and look at that and say, "Whew!
Surely I hardly matter. I am just a tiny little peek-
a-boo on this weird spot of dust called Earth, and all
that out there was going on billions of years before
I was born, and will still go on billions of years after
I die." Nothing may seem stranger to you than that —
more different from you. But there comes a point when
you will say, "Why, that's me!" And when you know
that, you know you never die.

5
DEATH, BIRTH
AND THE UNBORN

In this moment you are not born and you do not die. The you that is here now is never going to die, it will be an entirely different you who dies, sufficient unto the day as the trouble thereof. This idea is similar to the Heraclitus philosophy that you never step into the same stream twice, because it is a different stream each time. Likewise, in the early writings of Chinese Buddhist scholars:

> *"The sun in its course does not move.*
> *Every time it seems to move,*
> *it is a different sun."*

Today it is a very popular point of view among physicists that there is nothing moving around in the universe, that there is only motion, there is only pattern — no atoms of time and space. The Islamic people also have a theory about this; they say that God is creating the universe every instant. Just as frames of a movie give the illusion of motion, all instantly created universes in a series give the illusion that something is going along, but nothing is going along at all. The notion of there being a wave, a substantial peak of water moving along, is also an illusion, for the water is merely going up and down.

The Chinese word *wunien*, which we translate as 'no thought', has the meaning of not allowing a series of thoughts to link up in such a way that you become bound by the chain of continuity. Thus, the awareness of change is a matter of establishing continuities between moments. One could say there is no change, there is only the moment; or one could twist this around and say there are no substantial moments, the only real thing is flow. Both of these extreme points of view will induce the same state of consciousness. If on one hand you say there is only the here and now, and that is all you have to worry about, that will induce a state of consciousness which will be exactly the same state as induced by the feeling that everything is flow and nothing can hold it — so relax. Whether you are in the stream flowing with it, or sitting alongside the stream letting it go by, both illustrate the same sensation, only the metaphor is different.

Found in the Pali-Buddhist scriptures, in a book called *Itivuttaka*, is a phrase where Buddha says:

"There is an unborn, unoriginated, uncreated and unformed. Were there not, there would be no liberation from the world of the born, originated, created, and formed."

This theory of the unborn is embodied in the two Chinese characters, *fu-shy*; the first one 'not', and the second one, 'arising'. The idea of an unborn aspect of ourselves may seem odd to many people in the West. If someone asks, "Where do you think you are going when you die?", and someone answers, "I don't think I am going anywhere", a Westerner would ordinarily interpret this as meaning "I think I shall be totally annihilated, just blown out like a light and that will be that." The Zen meaning of this reply is: "I am not going anywhere when I die because I have never been born." You cannot die without being born any more than you can get divorced without being married. It is all a question of where you draw the line in defining who and what you are. Do you draw the line at just that much of you which you are aware of, just that much which your consciousness can catch hold of? Ordinarily, that is what we call our ego. The question is, how much of yourself can you catch hold of, and who is doing the catching? This aspect of you is unborn in the sense that nobody can ever catch hold of it, nobody can define it, nobody can give it a name, and nobody can pin it down. Yet, this is the really important aspect of you. In the case of the iceberg, only one seventh of it is above water. In our case, hardly anything at all is above water, just this little flicker of conscious attention with which we inspect the world, mostly in a linear fashion.

So, that which you do not know of yourself, and that which is never controlled by you in the way that you think you control things voluntarily, is the major, central part of you. This was the original truth in the astrological idea that when you drew a map of a person's soul you drew a map of the universe as it was centered upon the time and place of the individual nativity. I do not happen to believe very much in popular astrology, but there is this idea involved in it, which is that the soul is not something *in* the body, rather the body is something in the soul. The soul is not some individual spook, it is the whole network of relationships ranging throughout everything that there is. The "here and now" is like a knot in a system of strings making a fishing net, but the whole vast network is the soul. Everyone has the same soul, but we all experience it from different points of view, in different places, at different times. This soul that we all share is the totality of the whole process going on, and it keeps on going in us. Every single individual is a function of the whole energy. Whatever it is that is shining the sun is embodied in you. It is not something that happens to you. There is no seperate ego which is clobbered by this process. The feeling of being an ego *is* this process, and this means that your ego is not really an ego at all. It is a put-up job. It is a mask with which the whole thing is performing. You may say, "Well, I would like to get control of this thing, I feel sort of pushed around. All of this that is happening under the surface of my consciousness cannot be known, cannot be predicted, and isn't me." But this is merely an illusion. You have no need to object to being pushed around. There isn't anybody being pushed around except the whole system itself. It is pushing itself around, there are no victims. There is the *idea* that there are victims, the experience of *being* a victim, but this is again an illusion. The whole thing is an illusion in the sense of the old latin work *luderi*, meaning to play. It is playing at being in a mess; and you can only know what playing at being in fine shape is if you also know what playing in a mess is. We alternate, or vibrate, between these two extremes.

The point is that you, the you that is really doing it, is unborn and unknown. It is never an object of knowledge, and it is not something that you can catch hold of because you do not need to. Just as the sun does not need to shine on itself, a knife to cut itself, the eye to see itself, or the teeth to bite themselves, so all the way around, this whatever-it-is does not need to catch hold of itself and control itself.

Suppose that in order to pick up a pen with my thumb and forefinger I had to move the other fingers around and push that thumb and forefinger together so that they could pick up the pen. That would be kind of messy, wouldn't it? The hand doesn't have to catch hold of itself to control itself. The hand doesn't know how it controls itself, it just does it. The centipede can organize a hundred legs without having to think about it. So, in the same way, the Hindu gods do not know how they manage to be omnipotent; their myriads of arms are a symbol that the divine power does everything without explaining it and without having to know in terms of words how it is done. I assume the Christian God, who is supposed to be able to explain it all in words, is a big talker. "In the Beginning there was the Word..." — he would have to sit around for all eternity telling all those angels and saints how it was done. Words can only describe the singletracked, whereas, the universe is not single-tracked. It is everything happening everywhere, altogether, all at once. Words are too slow to keep track of that, and so we organize our bodies without having to think about it. If we had to think about it, we couldn't do it. I hear people say, "I don't do it, it happens to me." As though their body is an occurance that they find themselves mixed up with. That is absolutely backwards thinking. That is crazy. Your body *is* you; and you are a lot more than your body because your body is what is continuous with everything else that is going on as far as the farthest galaxies that can be concieved. It exists in and as a function of that whole situation. That is you.

Deepdown, fundamentally, you are the unborn. You never had a beginning and you do not have an end. You did not come into being and you never go out of being. What we call individual things, individual wiggles, individual waves, are pulses in the pattern; they come and they go. They are born and they die, and they are going all the time. But the whole thing, beyond these cycles of birth and death, is always there; and that is the unborn.

There was a Zen master of the seventeenth century in Japan named Bankei-Eitaku, who was enormously successful in conveying Zen to very simple people. He made a great point of the idea of the unborn, and of learning to trust the wisdom of the unconscious — that vast, limitless aspect of our nature which is totally beyond our control. Bankei is a notable person historically because he was the *roshi* of one of the greatest, most beautiful, Zen monasteries in Kyoto, Myoshinji. And he did a very interesting thing, in that he left no disciples or successors. Ordinarily, a Zen teacher passes his authority on to someone else, or to several people, and gives them his *inca*, which means seal of approval. This confirms that they have realized enlightenment under the master's guidance and are therefore authorized to teach in his school. But Bankei did not leave anyone, and this is considered a very fine accomplishment. It is said in a Zen poem of a wise man:

> Entering a forest he does not disturb
> a blade of grass, entering the water
> he does not make a ripple.

This saying goes back to the Buddha's own saying in the *Dhammapada*, that the path of the wise one is like the tracks of birds in the sky, nobody knows they have been around. Likewise, when you see a performance of a very great artist it looks absolutely uncontrived, as if it is happening naturally. Whatever discipline has gone into it, whatever skill, whatever learning, is not apparent. In the same way, when you construct a house you build scaffolding. When the time comes to finish the house all the scaffolding is taken down and vanishes.

The French philosopher, de Chardin, points out that in the course of evolution the peduncles disappear. Do you know what a peduncle is? When an amoeba splits, or when two globules of oil in a solution come out of one, first the original ball turns into an oval, like a capsule, and it gets thinner and thinner in the middle until it breaks apart and you have two tear-shaped forms. The little projections on the tear-shapes, the points, are peduncles. As the two globules drift apart they become oval again and the peduncles vanish. It may well be, for example, that all our roads, wires, and systems of communications are peduncles; that, if our civilization successfully continues, all roads will vanish, the wires will completely disappear, and eventually radio and electronics of all kinds will be unnecessary. People will communicate telepathically and we will feel ourselves to be one great organism. Who knows? The whole thing may be a peduncle which, after teaching us something, will simply vanish.

Newtonian mechanics, the idea that the universe can be explained by analogy with billiards, is a peduncle idea. Although it was an essential step that took us from one place to another, it has dropped away. We now have quantum mechanics instead. When you get the car, you drop the horse and buggy; when you get the plane, you drop the car; and when you become a star rover, then you drop the plane. So, to leave no trace is to leave no peduncle. This is always considered admirable in Zen character. Many masters might pride themselves on the number of disciples they have, but the really good teacher doesn't have any students. They all go away. They don't stick around and say, "Yes, well, I belong to the society that was created by (so-and-so)" and "I am a member of (such-and-such)." A really good teacher's students do not identify with that. To the extent that any religious teacher leaves behind disciples to carry on, they invariably ruin it. The original spirit of Christianity was completely destroyed by the disciples of Christ who organized it, boosted it, and so on. The smart teacher leaves no disciples. He helps all kinds of people, and to the degree that he helps them they are set free; they do no stick around. And this is what happened with this man, Bankei.

Bankei was a contemporary of Hakuin, another Zen master. Hakuin was a most remarkable and formidable man, but he left eighty disciples who are all on the books as having inherited his seal. Modern Zen in Japan is largely descended from Hakuin as his methods have prevailed. He used the way of koan study which is now used in the *Rinzai* sect. There is nothing wrong with this method, but Bankei's technique was very subtle.

The following is a talk that Bankei gave about the unborn mind:

> *The mind begotten by and given to each of us by our parents is none other than the Buddha-mind, birthless and immaculate, sufficient to manage all that life throws up to us.*
>
> *Suppose that at this very instant while you face me listening, a crow caws and a sparrow twitters somewhere behind you. Without any intention on your part to distinguish between these sounds, you hear each distinctly. Well, we are to be in this mind from now on, and our school will be known as the Buddha-mind school.... All of you are Buddhas because the birthless, which each possesses, is the beginning and the basis of all.*

Now, if the Buddha-mind is birthless, it is neces-sarily immortal. For, how can what has never been born perish? You have all encountered the phrase, 'birthless and imperishable' in the sutras, but hitherto you have not had the slightest proof of this truth. Indeed, I suppose like most people you have memorized this phrase while being ignorant of the fact of birthlessness. When I was twenty-five I realized that nonbirth is all-sufficient to life and since then, for forty years, I have been proving it to people just like you.

Bankei is saying that we all inherit the Buddha-mind, birthless and immaculate, which is "sufficient to manage all that life throws up to us." You can sit around and worry and prepare as to what you are going to do if you get in a very serious jam, but you have, auto-matically, an innate capacity to take care of the situation as and when it arises.

Let us suppose you are going to get cancer and you start to think about how you might react to that. Will you be able to endure it? Will you be able to do this, that, and the other? As you prepare a defensive attitude to this experience, you naturally get more and more worried. You may think, "Well, I don't want to be a coward. I don't want to appear to my friends to go to pieces and start screaming bloody murder, and I don't want to fall apart because that would be so un-diginfied. I hope I can end my days in a noble fashion and not be a nuisance to people." One can spend many nights awake with such thoughts, trying to get ready somehow. Although you may put money in the bank and have it there for a future eventuality, which is a kind of practical preparation, psychological preparation is a waste of time. When you are going into a very important interview and you think ahead of time how you are going to start out — what sort of ploy to use, and how you are going to speak to this person — it never works.

Jesus said a very curious thing to his disciples about preaching. He told them never to think in advance what they were going to say because at the right time the Holy Spirit would give it to them. In schools where they train clergymen to preach, they always concentrate on preparation. "Have three points: beginning, middle, and end; and know exactly where you are going." Obviously, they do not believe in the Holy Spirit! It is something that is all very well, but "Praise the Lord, and pass the ammunition!"

We have this total lack of being able to let it happen. This is not to say that one needs no training or discipline in anything, that is all very important, but every discipline that you learn, whether artistic or scientific, must always be subordinate to your spontaneity. Fundamentally, discipline is always to be at the disposal of something you do not know about and cannot control. For example, I have studied writing and speaking for years, but I never know what I am going to say next. It either happens or it doesn't. This is because it is being done by something that is not in my control at all. That is why Socrates used to say that he did not speak his philosophy but that there was a divine being that spoke through him.

All people who are creative in any way what-so-ever sometimes get the feeling that there is some other agency, that they are simply a secretary through which something happens. In the same way, when you reach a certain level of proficiency in playing a musical instrument, you start to get the feeling that the instrument is playing the music. Or, when you obtain a certain facility in using a brush, especially in writing Chinese characters, it suddenly seems the brush is an enchanted being which is carrying you away and using you to write characters. In singing, sometimes you can feel that the song is singing the singer. It is the strange feeling that it is happening by itself rather than that you are doing it. This is exactly why the Chinese use the phrase, *tzu-jan*, 'of itself so', for nature. *Tzu-jan* is the sensation of the world as something that is happening of itself — I am not doing it, and yet this thing that I am not doing is really me.

Why then, do people get so preoccupied with whether they are making spiritual or psychological progress? They worry as to whether they are really getting the point. Actually all this is a kind of acquisitiveness. You can turn it around and say, "I hope I have made progress in being nonacquisitive", and it is just the same thing, only backwards. Lao-tzu says that whereas the scholar is a man who gains something everyday, a Taoist is a man who loses something everyday. A scholar is interested in acquiring and accumulating knowledge, a Taoist is interested in getting rid of knowledge. Not literally becoming a moron, but becoming free from fixed views of the world. This often leads to a funny sort of competition. Can I lose my mind faster than you? Can I get rid of more concepts everyday than you can? All this is simply the mirror image of the guy who is playing the one-up-manship of acquisition. Always watch out for these games. There are the most unbelievably subtle competitions going on. Such as: I am more tolerant than you are (that is a great game); or, I am more aware than you are of how dreadful I am; or, I am more aware than you are of how many games I am playing. You can follow this out and suddenly find yourself in a devil of a situation because you find that there is no way of not playing competitive games. You are in one whatever you do. When you understand that, then you do not play the most awful of all games which is: "you are playing games but I am not." When you know that there is nothing else to do except play competitive games, then you suddenly realize that you are not in the trap but that you *are* the trap. As soon as you are the trap, there is no trap, because it takes something to be trapped for there to be a trap.

When Bankei says, "Buddha-mind", it is his particular phrase for the unconcious. This is not the psychological unconscious of Freud and Jung, but that total aspect of ourselves of which we are ignore-ant, and which does not come into the focus of conscious attention because it stands behind it. He also says that the Buddha-mind in each of you is immaculate. Be careful of this word 'immaculate'. In the West, in Christianity, we use words like 'pure', 'immaculate', and 'spotless' to mean sexless. When it is said, "Blessed are the pure in heart for they shall see God", most people think that a pure-minded person is one who does not tell dirty jokes or have lustful thoughts. Pure, *catharo* is Greek, means clear. The meaning here is pure like space, which is clear like a mirror or a crystal.

A mirror will reflect piles of dung and all kinds of obscenities, but this doesn't affect the mirror. Chuang-tzu says of the mirror, "It grasps nothing, it refuses nothing. It receives but does not keep; therefore, it is never stained. It has no color; therefore, it reflects all colors." The Buddha-mind is like a mirror — all you do is reflect in it; and all you do is reflected in it. If you bother about one reflection, you are certain to go astray.

Your thoughts do not lie deep enough. They rise from the shallows of you mind. Bankei writes:

> *Remember that all you see and hear is reflected in the Buddha-mind and influenced by what was previously seen and heard. Needless to say, thoughts are not entities. If you permit them to rise and reflect themselves, or cease altogether, as they are prone to do — if you do not worry about them, you will never go astray. In this way, let one hundred, nay, one thousand thoughts arise, and it is as if not one has arisen — You will remain undisturbed.*

This is saying, "Get to the point!" the past which you are remembering and reacting to and bitching about simply is not here. Most arguments between people are about things which are not happening. They are about things which have happened and might happen, but not about things which are happening. It is absolutely fascinating, as a psychotheraputic technique, to bring someone to the present and say, "Where do you hurt?" Especially if it is a psychological ache — "Where is it? What is it like? Tell me, in this moment do you have a problem?" People start looking around and around, and they cannot find the darn thing.

It is like the famous story of Bodhidharma and Hui-k'e, his disciple. Hui-k'e was so determined to get the truth of Zen from Bodhidharma that he cut off his left arm and presented it to Bodhidharma saying:

"This is a token of my sincerity", and Bodhidharma finally said, "Alright, alright, what is troubling you?" Hui-k'e said, "Well, I have no peace of mind, please pacify my mind", and Bodhidharma said, "Bring out your mind here before me, I will pacify it". Hui-k'e replied, "Well, when I look for it I cannot find it", and Bodhidharma said, "There, it is pacified."

Fundamentally, this is the way Zen works. Find that ego which you are in trouble about, that you are afraid of losing when you die. Find it, put your finger on it, bring it out. Where is it? What is your problem? You look for it and you can't find it because it is an abstraction. It is something that exists in a world of words and symbols, and has no physical reality what-so-ever.

In another passage Bankei says:

The only thing I tell my people is to stay in the Buddha-mind. There are no regulations, no formal disciplines. Nevertheless, they have agreed among themselves to sit in Zen, that is, practice za-zen, for a period of two incense sticks daily. Alright, let them. But they should well understand that the birthless Budha-mind has absolutely nothing to do with sitting with an incense stick burning in front of you.

If one keeps in the Buddhamind without straying, there is no further satori to seek. Whether awake or asleep, one is living Buddha.

Za-zen means only one thing: sitting tranquilly in the Buddha-mind. But really, you know, one's everyday life in its entirety should be thought of as sitting in Zen. Even during one's formal sitting, one may leave one's seat to attend to something. A natural thing, after all. One cannot sleep all day so one rises, one cannot walk all day so one sits in Zen. There are no binding rules here.

Most masters these days use devices to teach and these devices they seem to value above all else. They cannot get to the truth directly. They are little more than blind fools.

Another bit of stupidity of theirs, is to hold that, according to Zen, unless one has a doubt which he proceeds to smash, he is good for nothing. Of course, all this forces people to have doubts. No, they never teach the importance of staying in the birthless Buddha-mind. They would make of it a lump of doubts; it is a very serious mistake.

This man Bankei, was really something. What he is saying is actually terribly heretical. When he talks about the doubt, he is referring one of the techniques in Zen which stirs up an intense anxiety in a person, as well as a feeling of total spiritual insufficiency. This is a trick of the five-day sessions where they meditate most of the day and the teacher works up more and more a sense of frustration. Bankei makes the point that people who went to a teacher and deliberately got themselves into the state of the great doubt, were doing something artificial. In other words, if you want to feel very, very free, why don't you put lead in your shoes for a month and go around that way. After a month take it out and you'll feel great! This is also the way revivalists work. They get a bunch of people together and convince them that they are absolute, awful sinners. They go at it, and go at it, until the people feel so guilty that they don't know where to turn. Then having made them sick, they say, "Ah, but I have the medicine! Just put yourself completely in Jesus Christ, come forward here, and let it all go to Jesus." And so, he saves them from their sins and everybody is immensely relieved. It is like a person who goes and sits on someone and then gets up — that is all he has done. There is a kind of phony spirituality about this, but there is alot of it going on in organized church religions, and it also goes on in Zen.

Bankei, however, saw through this spiritual pretense. He was trying to say, "Look, there is not any fixed way of practicing Zen. Everything is Zen practice, everything is meditation. The essential art of the whole thing is to realize that you can depend on that vast aspect of yourself which you know nothing about. That is the Buddha-mind." The same thing is true of all religions and philosophies. Christian Scientists, for example, say that if you have faith you will be healed. But then faith becomes something that you somehow ought to do.

Bankei is not saying that, and this is very important. He is saying that you can have all the doubts you want to have, and all the mistrust you want to have in your deepest self, but do not put faith in it because it does not make the slightest difference. You cannot get away from it. One way is saying: to get to something, there is something special you ought to do, whether it is a kind of doing, or giving up; the other is saying: no, there is nothing you have to do because you are it. You are this thing functioning, this cosmic energy dancing in the form of you. From a particularly personal point of view you may be doing as well or as badly as may be, but there is nothing you can do to be other than that. It is like walking on the ground and the ground is holding you up. You are at liberty to suppose that it will collapse under your feet at any moment, but the truth is, it still goes on holding you up.

THE PRACTICE
OF MEDITATION

The practice of meditation is not what is ordinarily meant by practice, in the sense of repetitious preparation for some future performance. It may seem odd and illogical to say that meditation in the form of yoga, dhyana, or za-zen, as used by Hindus and Buddhists, is a practice without purpose—in some future time—because it is the art of being completely centered in the here and now. "I'm not sleepy, and there is no place I'm going to."

We are living in a culture entirely hypnotized by the illusion of time, in which the so-called present moment is felt as nothing but an infinitesimal hairline between an all-powerfully causative past and an absorbingly important future. We have no present. Our consciousness is almost completely preoccupied with memory and expectation. We do not realize that there never was, is, or will be any other experience than present experience.

We are therefore out of touch with reality. We confuse the world as talked about, described, and measured with the world which actually is. We are sick with a fascination for the useful tools of names and numbers, of symbols, signs, conceptions, and ideas. Meditation is therefore the art of suspending verbal and symbolic thinking for a time, somewhat as a courteous audience will stop talking when a concert is about to begin.

Simply sit down, close your eyes, and listen to all sounds that may be going on—without trying to name or identify them. Listen as you would listen to music. If you find that verbal thinking will not drop away, don't attempt to stop it by force of will-power. Just keep your tongue relaxed, floating easily in the lower jaw, and listen to your thoughts as if they were birds chattering outside—mere noise in the skull—and they will eventually subside of themselves, as a turbulent and muddy pool will become calm and clear if left alone.

Also, become aware of breathing and allow your lungs to work in whatever rhythm seems congenial to them. And for a while just sit listening and feeling breath. But, if possible, don't _call_ it that. Simply experience the non-verbal happening. You may object that this is not "spiritual" meditation but mere attention to the "physical" world, but it should be understood that the spiritual and the physical are only ideas, philosophical conceptions, and that the reality of which you are now aware is not an idea. Furthermore, there is no "you" aware of it. That was also just an idea. Can you hear yourself listening?

And then begin to let your breath "fall" out, slowly and easily. Don't force or strain your lungs, but let the breath come out in the same way that you let yourself slump into a comfortable bed. Simply let

it go, go, and go. As soon as there is the least
strain, just let it come back in as a reflex; don't
pull it in. Forget the clock. Forget to count. Just
keep it up for so long as you feel the luxury of it.

Using the breath in this way, you discover how to
generate energy without force. For example, one of
the gimmicks [in Sanskrit, upaya] used to quiet
the thinking mind and its compulsive chattering is
known as mantra — the chanting of sounds for the
sake of sound rather than meaning. Therefore begin
to "float" a single tone on the long, easy outbreath
at whatever pitch is most comfortable. Hindus and
Buddhists use for this practice such syllables as
ŌM, AH, HUM [i.e. HUNG], and Christians might
prefer AMEN or ALLELUIA, Muslims ALLAH, and
Jews ADONAI: it really makes no difference, since
what is important is simply and solely the sound.
Like Zen Buddhists, you could use just the syllable
MOOO [###]. Dig that, and let your consciousness
sink down, down, down into the sound for as long
as there is no sense of strain.

Above all, don't look for a result, for some
marvellous change of consciousness or Satori: the
whole essence of meditation-practice is centering
upon what IS — not on what should or might be.
The point is not to make the mind blank or to

concentrate fiercely upon, say, a single point of light — although that, too, can be delightful without the fierceness.

For how long should this be kept up? My own, and perhaps unorthodox, feeling is that it can be continued for as long as there is no sensation of forcing it — and this may easily extend to 30 or 40 minutes at one sitting, whereafter you will want to return to the state of normal restlessness and distraction.

In sitting for meditation, it is best to use a substantial cushion on the floor, to keep the spine erect but not stiff, to have the hands on the lap — palms upwards — resting easily upon each other, and to sit cross-legged like a Buddha-figure, either in full or half "lotus" posture, or kneeling and sitting back on the heels. "Lotus" means placing one or both feet sole upwards upon the opposite thigh. These postures are slightly uncomfortable, but they have, therefore, the advantage of keeping you awake!

In the course of meditation you may possibly have astonishing visions, amazing ideas, and fascinating fantasies. You may also feel that you are becoming clairvoyant or that you are able to leave your body and travel at will. But all that is distraction. Leave it alone and simply watch what happens NOW. One does not meditate in order to acquire extraordinary powers, for if you managed to become omnipotent and omniscient, what would you do? There would be no further surprises for you, and your whole life would be like making love to a plastic woman. Beware, then, of all those gurus who promise "marvellous results" and other future benefits from their disciplines. The whole point is to realize that there _is_ no future, and that the real sense of life is an exploration of the eternal now. STOP, LOOK, and LISTEN! Or shall we say, "Turn on, tune in, and drop _in_"?

A story is told of a man who came to the Buddha with offerings of flowers in both hands. The Buddha said, "Drop it!" So he dropped the flowers in his left hand. The Buddha said again "Drop it!" He dropped the flowers in his right hand. And the Buddha said, "Drop that which you have neither in the right nor in the left, but in the middle!" And the man was instantly enlightened.

It is marvellous to have the sense that all living and moving is dropping, or going along with gravity. After all—the earth is falling around the sun, and, in turn, the sun is falling around some other star. For energy is precisely a taking of the line of least resistance. Energy is mass. The power of water is in following its own weight. All comes to him who weights.